Author's Note:

Even though alliteration (explained on the back cover) deals with same sounds, I decided to create a book using the alphabet. Before beginning your journey through the alphabet sounds, please explain to your child very simply that each letter has a sound, and that sound will be repeated in each sentence. I've tried to include animals that your child may not be too familiar with, so that could also be a lesson in itself. A good idea in expanding our learning experience could be researching that particular animal and then discussing it with your child.

I hope your child gains something positive from this book.

A-Z SOUNDS WITH ALLITERATION

A Z

SOUNDS WITH ALLITERATION

By Zeena Musallam - Kandalaft

Illustrated by Sara Bdeir

A

Amy **a**nd **A**llen **a**re watching **an** **a**nteater eat **a**nts with its long tongue.

Babu and **B**ina look at a **b**ig **b**rown **b**ear **b**ouncing a **b**all near
a **b**ucket of **b**lue paint.

C

Coco the **c**at and her **c**ute kittens **c**limb the **c**oconut tree using their **c**laws.

Daniel's **d**og **D**igger **d**igs holes **d**aily in his **d**affodil garden.

Elena the **e**lephant catches **e**leven fish because of her **e**xcellent **e**yesight.

Fred the **f**riendly **f**isherman holds a **f**lat **f**lounder **f**ish.

G

Gary the **g**rumpy **g**reen **g**ecko walks up the **g**rey **g**arbage can onto a **g**lass window.

Harry the **h**ilarious **h**orse lifts **h**is **h**ead up **h**igh, **h**appy with **h**is **h**andsome mane of **h**air.

Imad the **i**guana **i**magines his **i**nvisible friend **I**vy with **i**ndigo colored wings.

Jack the **j**olly giant **j**ogs to see **j**iggly **j**ellyfish.

Karma the **k**oala and **K**arim the **k**angaroo
love to fly cookie **k**ites.

Lily the ladybug lives on leaves near Lollipop Lake.

M

Mustafa the **m**assive **m**anatee is a slow **m**oving **m**arine **m**ammal who eats **m**any plants.

Natalie the **n**arwhal and her **n**ine **n**oisy **n**ieces have long and **n**arrow **n**eedle-like teeth.

O

Omar the **o**ctopus and **O**lga the **o**yster dance with **O**sey the **o**rca in the **o**cean.

P

Pearl the **p**roud **p**eacock **p**rincess **p**lucks
a **p**urple feather off her tail.

Quin the **q**uagga looks **q**uite **q**uirky.

Ramzi sees a **r**eindeer swim the **r**iver **r**apids in the **r**ain.

S

Suzie the **s**illy **s**eal likes to **s**wim in the **s**ea and **s**plash **s**eagulls.

T

Tina the **t**arsier may be **t**iny, but her eyes are **t**itanic.

Unlucky **U**no steps on an **u**rchin that lives **u**nder an **u**mbrella in the sea.

Vern the **v**ampire is **v**ery careful around **V**iolet the **v**iper.

Wendy sees a **w**obbly **w**alrus **w**ith long **w**hite tusks **w**inking at her.

X

(The x sounds like z.) **X**avier and **X**ia see a strange looking **x**enopus frog playing a **x**ylophone in a pond.

Yama the **y**oung **y**eti throws egg **y**olks at a group of **y**ellow **y**aks doing **y**oga.

Zoe the **z**ebra dreams of a **z**ombie **z**ipping through space.

Did you

enjoy

reading

this book?

If so, then there are more to follow:

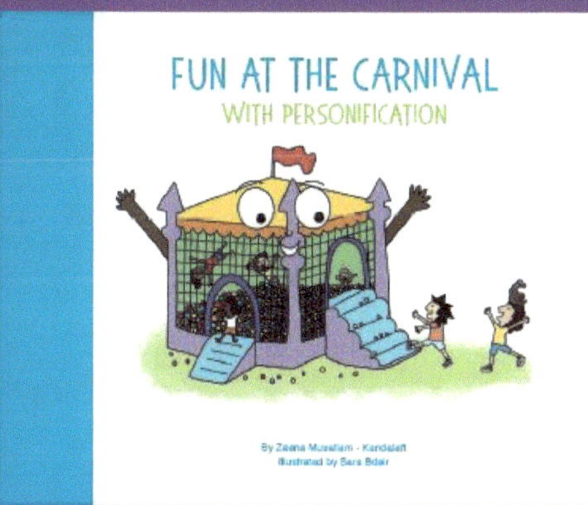

Join Pedro and Suki on a fun day at the carnival, and watch the carnival come to life with personification.

Playing pranks is always fun especially with Sami and Salma. Learn how to use similes by using the words **like** or **as**.

This book includes short pieces that come together in the very end. It is a metaphor lesson, and a lesson on bullying and having self-confidence.

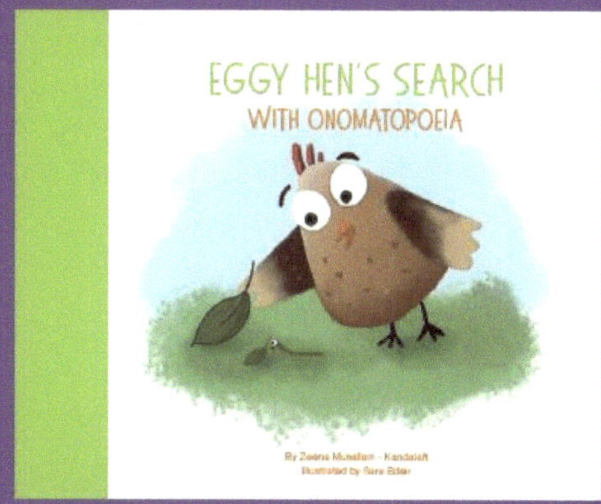

Follow Eggy Hen search for her missing eggs, and listen to all the sounds on the farm with the help of onomatopoeia.